What's the Weather?

IT'S WINDY!

By Alex Appleby

Gareth Stevens Publishing

Please visit our website, www.garethstevens.com. For a free color catalog of all our high-quality books, call toll free 1-800-542-2595 or fax 1-877-542-2596.

Library of Congress Cataloging-in-Publication Data

Appleby, Alex.
It's windy! / by Appleby, Alex.
p. cm. – (What's the weather)
Includes index.
ISBN 978-1-4339-9413-5 (pbk.)
ISBN 978-1-4339-9414-2 (6-pack)
ISBN 978-1-4339-9412-8 (library binding)
1. Winds — Juvenile literature. I. Appleby, Alex. II. Title.
QC931.4 N34 2014
551.518—dc23

First Edition

Published in 2014 by
Gareth Stevens Publishing
111 East 14th Street, Suite 349
New York, NY 10003

Editor: Ryan Nagelhout
Designer: Andrea Davison-Bartolotta

All illustration by Michael Harmon

Printed in the United States of America

CPSIA compliance information: Batch #CS13GS: For further information contact Gareth Stevens, New York, New York at 1-800-542-2595.

Contents

It is windy!

The wind moves clouds over my head.

The elm tree in my yard
is shaking.

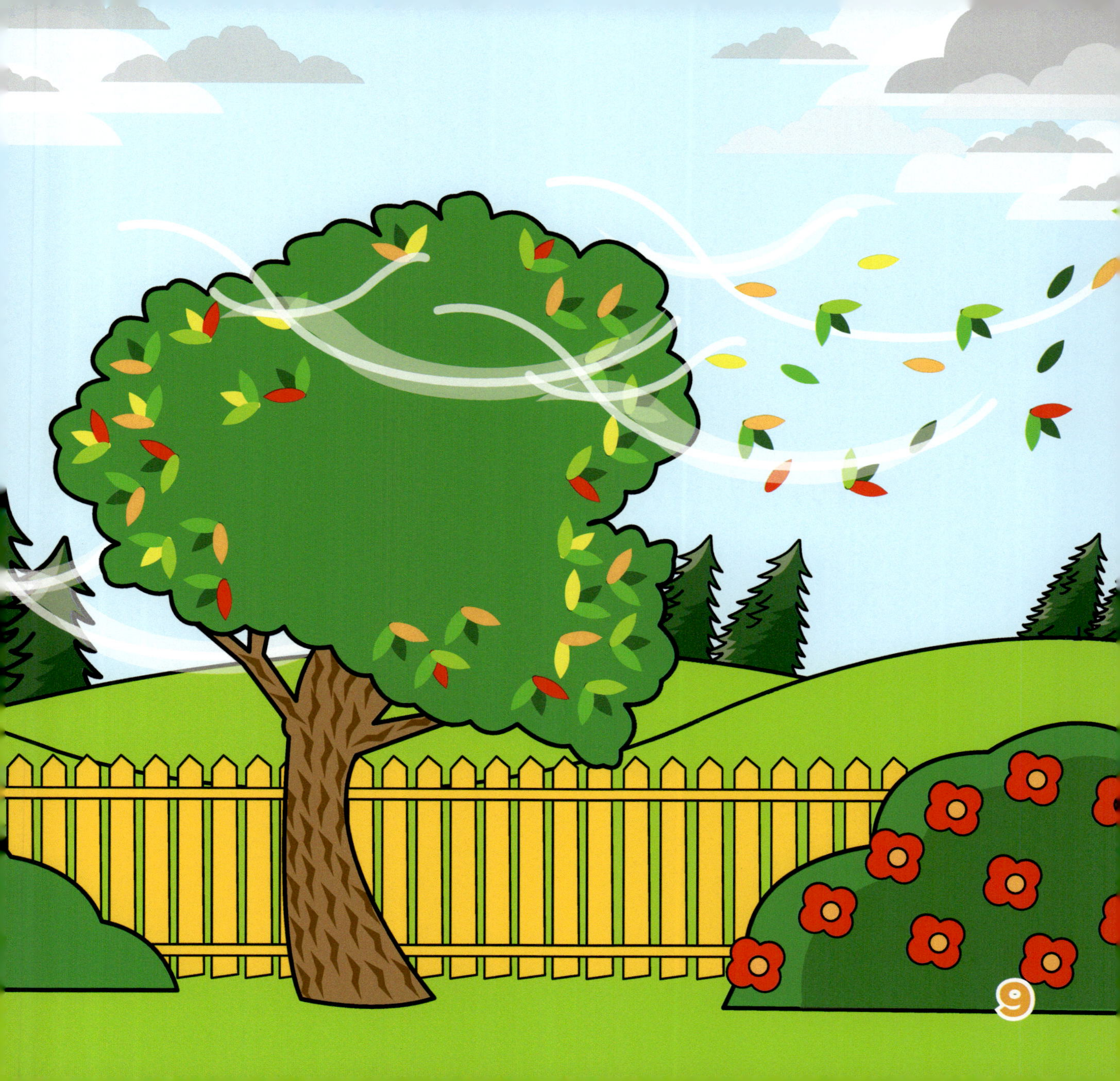

Wind makes it feel colder outside.

I wear a blue jacket
when it's windy.

Winds can be strong!
This is called a gust.

It blows off my blue hat!

I chase after my hat.
It lands in a green bush.

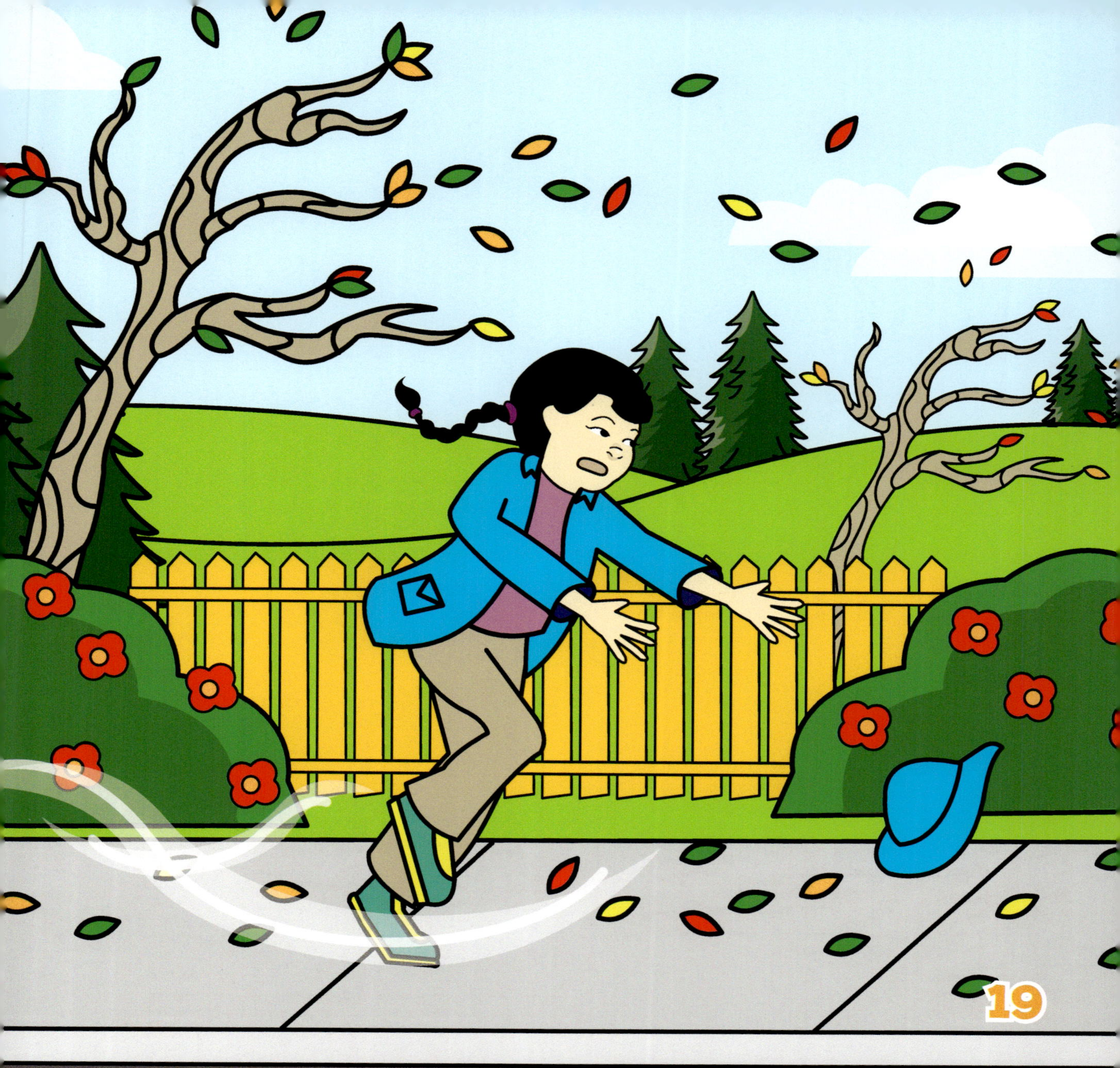

Other winds are lighter.
This is a breeze.

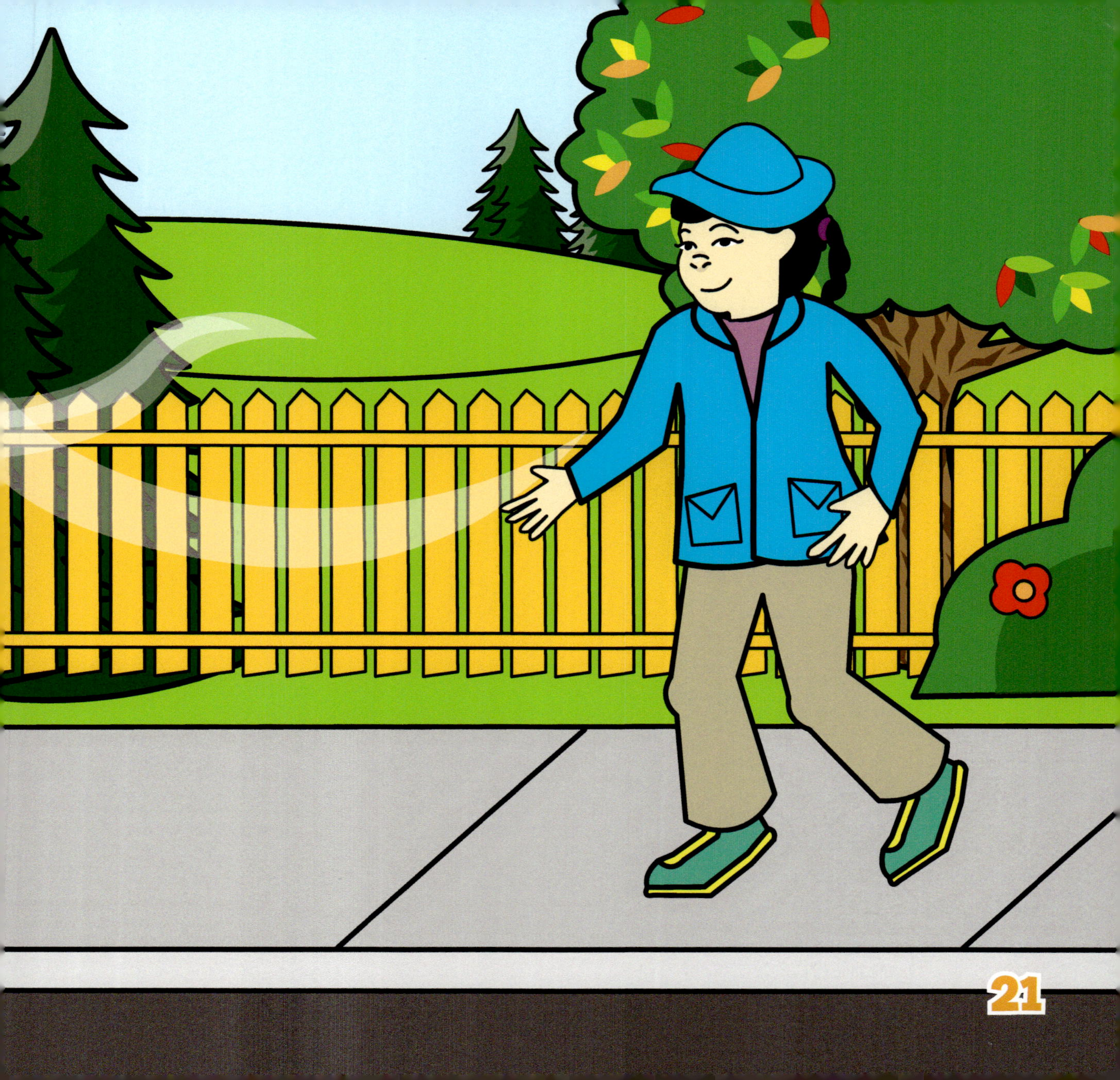

The wind helps me fly my red kite!

Words to Know

bush

clouds

elm tree

Index